Detection of Trapped Victims in Disaster Scenarios using IoT

An IoT Based System to Detect the Trapped Victims in Disaster Scenarios using Doppler Microwave and Passive Infrared Technology

T VEERAMANIKANDASAMY

Assistant Professor
Department of Electronics and Communication Systems
Sri Krishna Arts and Science College
Coimbatore – 641 008

R DEEPA

Assistant Professor
Department of Electronics and Communication Science
D.R.B.C.C.C Hindu College
Chennai – 600 072

About the Authors

T Veeramanikandasamy is an Assistant Professor of Electronics and Communication Systems at Sri Krishna Arts and Science College, Coimbatore 641 008. He obtained his Doctorate degree in Electronics from Bharathiar University, Coimbatore, India. He has 13 years of teaching experience. His current research interests are in Nanomaterials Characterization, Embedded Systems, and Digital Signal Processing. He has published 11 research papers in peer-reviewed international journals. He has presented more than 16 research papers in national/international conferences. He has delivered more than 10 technical lectures in various institutions. He is a Life member of the Indian Society of Systems for Science and Engineering (ISSE). He received a certificate in Embedded Software Engineer (NSQF-QP ELE/Q1501) from Electronics Sector Skills Council of India (ESSCI). He has developed various student enrichment courses on Embedded Systems, Digital System Design, Digital Signal Processing, Programmable Logic Controller and IoT with Python.

R Deepa holds M.Phil in Electronics from Sri Krishna Arts and Science College, Coimbatore affiliated to Bharathiar University Coimbatore and M.Sc in Electronics and Communication Systems from Sri Krishna Arts and Science College, Coimbatore. She works in the Department of Electronics and Communication Science, Bhaktavatsalam Memorial College for Women, Chennai as an assistant professor and has five years of experience in the areas of teaching and administrative works.

CONTENTS

LIST OF FIGURES

LIST OF TABLES

LIST OF ABBREVIATIONS

IoT	Internet of Things
PIR	Passive Infra-Red Sensor
PIC	Peripheral Interface Controller
RADAR	Radio Detection and Ranging
Wi-Fi	Wireless Fidelity
LCD	Liquid Crystal Display
PCB	Printed Circuit Board
MEMS	Micro Electro Mechanical Systems
Tx/Rx	Transmitter & Receiver
LNA	Local Network Attachment
IDE	Integrated Development Environment
GUI	Graphical User Interface

PREFACE

The disasters are very hard to control and hard to save the people who are trapped under the rubbles apart from the damages caused. The presented work provides a highly sophisticated method for rescuing trapped victims during the disaster. The main objective is to communicate the information from different sensors to the webserver using the Internet of Things (IoT). The sensor modules used in the system are Microwave Doppler Radar Sensor, PIR Sensor, Bomb sensor, and Gas sensor.

New revolutionary technologies called Microwave Doppler and Passive Infrared are used for detecting the presence of humans in this proposed system. The system enables an easier way in the detection of alive human beings by extracting the heartbeat signals by using the Microwave Doppler Radar sensor. The Pyroelectric sensor uses the Passive Infrared technology which is incorporated with the Microwave Doppler radar to reduce the false indication of human presence. A bomb sensor and gas sensor modules are added for ensuring a safe rescue of trapped victims. The bomb sensor detects the presence of metals/bombs at the place of disaster. In the same way, the presence of any hazardous gas is detected using the gas sensor. The collected parameters of victims are displayed on a web server using IoT which makes it easier for monitoring victims from the central monitoring station.

Anyone can get to know about the victims from any part of the world. The main aim of IoT based detection of trapped victims in disaster scenarios using Doppler microwave and PIR technologies is to save the number of people from adverse conditions.

This book comprises eight chapters that are focused on the design of an IoT based system to detect trapped victims in disaster scenarios using Doppler microwave and passive infrared technology. Chapter 1 presents the introduction of the proposed system. Chapter 2 intends to review the published works regarding rescue operations in a disaster zone. Chapter 3 deals with the design and the real-time implementation of hardware for the detection of trapped victims in disaster scenarios. Chapter 4 presents the hardware detail and its working principles. Chapter 5 covers a methodology to develop source code for the entire system implementation. Chapter 6 is showing the simulation results of the discussed rescue operation. The rest of the chapters describe the future enhancement and conclusion of the proposed system.

CHAPTER - 1

INTRODUCTION

The technological era has a rapid growth that increases day by day making our life easier and comfortable to live. These technological developments have helped us in predicting the future of mankind. In that way, technological development has a solution for the disasters happening in the world either it is a manmade disaster or natural disaster. Even though the predictions are made no one can stop the disasters from happening. Nature brings disaster to mankind in a higher range by causing earthquakes, volcanic eruptions, floods, etc.

All these disasters are caused due to various geographical changes faced by the earth. Earthquakes, Volcanic eruptions are caused due to the movement of the earth's surface. Cyclones, Storms, Tornadoes are some weather-related disasters that are caused a higher level of damage. On the other hand, human beings create a disaster in the name of terrorism and war. The Bomb blast and some other terrorist attacks can create a major fire accident or collapse of buildings.

On seeing the history of India many disasters have occurred: The Indian Ocean erupted with heavy aggression in the year 2004 causing much loss of life and property in India, and neighboring countries like Sri Lanka and Indonesia. The 26 January 2001 disaster can never be forgotten by the people of India where Gujarat experienced a massive earthquake with a higher rate of the Richter scale of 7.6 to 7.9 in 2 minutes making more than 20,000 people lose their life. Another flood-hit Kashmir in 2014 leads to the death of 500 people. "The Human Cost of Weather-Related Disasters" a recent report by UN states that between the year 1995-2015 more than 2.3 billion people were affected by the flood, and flood occupies 56% of weather-related disasters which is the highest rate. Some induced disasters are also caused by coal mine extractions, Industrial accidents, etc. These disasters panic people as they cause a major loss of human life and also it becomes a nightmare for people involved in the rescue operation for saving the life of people stuck under the rubble of the building. This proposed system is mainly designed for the rescue of people who are stuck under the broken pieces of buildings and also to ensure a safe way for the rescue team to carry out their rescue safely and securely.

IoT (Internet of Things) is connected here with disaster management as in this era of social age everything is connected with the Internet, and according to global internet usage, 51% of the population in the world uses the Internet. Nowadays, IoT plays a main role in the healthcare system and many automation systems. Here in disaster management, the data collected at the field can be interconnected with the Internet for Data Management and analysis of data for future records. Internet of things is a system where physical objects are connected together and they are made accessible through the internet (Fig.1.1). The 'thing' present in IoT can be any heart monitor or detectors or built-in-sensors, etc.

The term 'thing' represents any object that has an IP address and any data can be transferred through the IP address without any manual assistance. Embedded technology present in the object helps them to interact with the Internet. Internet is used by the majority of the population in the world anything digitally connected with the internet makes work easier, control of devices can be done from any part of the world. It ensures increasing efficiency, safety, and security.

Internet of things has developed from wireless technologies, micro-electromechanical systems (MEMS), microservices and the internet. The development has helped in breaking down the barrier between the Operational technologies (OT) and Information technology (IT). This created an easier path for knowing the data generated by the machine.

Fig.1.1. Internet of Things

The Internet of things has a wide area of application in various fields. With the increasing use of the Internet by the people, everything becomes more fast and easier. Some of the advantages of using IoT are listed below,

- Efficient connectivity
- Analyzing data and action made immediately
- Integrate and transfer data in a faster way

- Improved decision making
- Design, develop and integrate IoT system
- Deploy and manage end to end IoT processes
- Integrate IoT with the existing architecture

The architecture of an IoT explains the sensing of the data at the ground level (Fig.1.2). The data are sensed from any physical devices and later they are transmitted to the next level for communicating with wireless sensor networks. The Internet of things plays an important role in critical environments like a disaster.

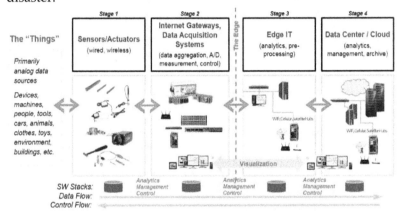

Fig.1.2. Layered Architecture of IoT

Every device is connected with the Internet and a new revolution can be made by using IoT in disaster management. IoT can create a great impact in this world with the advancement of technologies available to us. Everything comes to our hand within seconds; the whole network can be controlled in a single touch.

These advantages can be implemented in the right way to help people during disaster time. The speed, response time and quality of rescue operation can be increased. IoT offers great help in the preparation, prevention and recovery phases during the disaster. Some of the applications include

- A real-time sensor-based data about the place of disaster can be a revolutionary attempt.

- Forests and other wildlife environments can be interlinked with sensors for protecting wildlife.
- Any hazardous chemicals causing pollution in the environment can be monitored and all the data can be kept as a record using data management.
- Situational awareness and Incident management of a particular disaster can be made accessible by anyone.

PIC16F family microcontrollers are used in this system as it has a FLASH memory technology. In this, we can write-erase the chip until a thousand times. It can perform many tasks due to its large enough programming memory organization. PIC16F877A has a 40 pin path and out of which 33 I/Os used for many applications starting from the controlling of home appliances to the higher-level industrial instruments. It offers a low power consumption that makes it ideal for smart devices as well as battery-operated devices. EEPROM memory makes it easier to be used in devices where permanent storage of various parameters is needed. The features of PIC16F877A like flexibility and low cost make it applicable in areas where microcontrollers had not been previously considered like timer functions, interface replacement in larger systems, coprocessor applications, etc.

Doppler microwave technology uses the principle of detecting humans beyond the rubble by passing on the microwave signals. This is based upon the principle discovered by Christian Doppler in which the observed frequency of a wave depends upon the relative speed experienced by the movement of source and receiver; this is known as the Doppler Effect. In a Doppler radar system, a signal of known frequency is transmitted from the transmitting antenna which is received by the receiver and the signals are reflected back again with some modulated signals. The Doppler module has a built-in oscillator used to generate frequency.

The output wave is sinusoid in nature and contains a frequency which is the difference between the transmitted and received signal. A microwave beam is transmitted through the rubble at a particular portion under the collapsed building. This wave identifies the targets and reflects again with some modulated signal that is created due to the movement of the person that arises due to the heartbeat rate and breathing rate of the person.

In this system, a proper analysis is done for receiving the signal and identifying the presence of the alive human. The person can be rescued from a collapsed building anywhere at any time. The frequency of the heartbeat of the detected person is monitored by using a Microwave HB100 radar sensor. The life of the people who rescue the victims is very important as the life of the victims. Having this into consideration based on the cause and area of the collapsed building, the bomb detector and gas sensor are added to the module. All sensor data are interfaced with PIC16F MCU, and then the entire data are stored in a global system using IoT. The main purpose of interfacing the data with IoT is that the data of recovered people and the rescue operation can be recorded continuously.

CHAPTER - 2

REVIEW OF LITERATURE

Many researchers have tried various methods of object field monitoring using various technologies. Some of the research works which have been done in this field are abstracted below.

K.M.Chen, Y. Huang, A.Norman and J.Zhang proposed a system "Microwave life detection system for detecting human subjects through barriers". It focuses on the concept of the detection of buried victims using microwave beams. This system gave the idea that human presence can be detected using microwave beams. The change in heartbeat movements can be detected using this system. W.S.Haddad gave the idea of Rubble rescue radar for the detection of trapped human personnel.

David W Paglieroni, Christian T Pechard, and N Reginald Beer proposed "Change Detection in Constellations of Buried Objects Extracted from Ground-Penetrating Radar Data". In this system the GPR is used to identify the Object, the GPR deducts the object and the captured object is converted into a 3D image by Digital image processing. Here the objects are found, if we use this system in collapsed buildings, it denotes the objects and gives intimation to us.

G.Prabhakar Reddy, M.Vijayalakshmi designed IoT in mines for safety and efficient monitoring using IEEE802.11 Wi-Fi module wireless radio frequency communication. This gave an idea about sensing the data through the Wi-Fi module and sending the data to a web server.

Karthikeyan.S, Karthick. C and Shibu Prasath S.V. proposed the design of the "Human Tracking system for victims trapped from collapsed building". The objective of this system is the usage of multiple PIR sensors connected to PIC MCU for detecting the presence of humans under a collapsed building.

Nadia Binti Baharuddin evaluated a system of "An analysis of heartbeat monitoring using microwave Doppler technique". This work gave an idea of analyzing the heartbeat using microwave signals and the Doppler method. The study of monitoring the heartbeat without contact with the person is done here and this enables us to study the wireless transmission of heart signals.

Sandeep Bhatia presented work on "Alive human body detection system using an autonomous rescue robot" which proposes a new approach for detecting alive humans in destructed environments using an autonomous robot. Here the sensors are used for underground environment monitoring and automatic evolution of measurement data through digital wireless communication technique is proposed with high accuracy, smooth control, and reliability.

A review on ground penetrating radar technology for the detection of buried or trapped victims by Lorenzo Crocco and Vincenzo Ferrara. The heartbeat and breath are received by GPR. This system gave an idea about detecting the human beyond the rubbles of building.

Prajakta Sathe, Neha Poojary, Archana Shithole, S.V.Bhise presented the "Advanced Surveillance Robot" that used a video surveillance system to view the trapped humans. This system considered remote sensing as safer than any other technique.

Geetha bharathi.V.S, Sudha.S proposed "Alive human detection in disaster zones using manually controlled robots". They used a method of Human detection using a PIR sensor. The data are transferred using a Bluetooth module. The area of coverage was a matter of discussion in this system.

Shwetha.R, Chethan HK done work on "Automatic and manually controlled Alive human detection Robot using disaster management". This work used an economical robot that works using AVR MCU and PIR sensor. By sensing the human body temperature using a PIR sensor, the data is sent to mobile phones using GSM technology for enabling the rescue operation.

Mauricio Correa, Gabriel Hermollia, Rodrigo Verschee, Javier Ruiz proposed "Human Detection and Identification by Robots using Thermal and Visual Information in Domestic Environments". This is an intelligent system in which the presence of humans was detected by analyzing the thermal and visual information. These sources were integrated and then processed.

M. Vijayalakshmi and K. Rajalakshmi proposed a work which describes "On-Time Assist for Victims Trapped in Collapsed Building Enhanced with IOT Technology". This system detected the human presence using a Piezoelectric sensor. Here the idea about sensing the data and sending them to a web server page was studied.

CHAPTER – 3

SYSTEM IMPLEMENTATION

3.1. BLOCK DIAGRAM

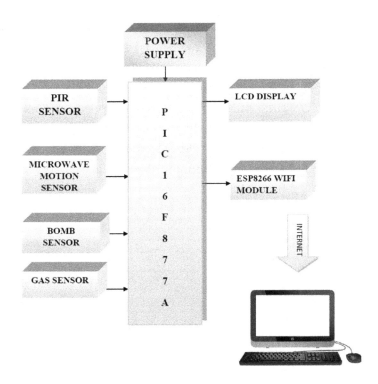

Fig.3.1. Block diagram of IoT based System for the Detection of Trapped Victims in Disaster Scenarios

3.2. BLOCK DIAGRAM DESCRIPTION

The project "An IoT Based System to Detect the Trapped Victims in Disaster Scenarios using Doppler Microwave and Passive Infrared Technology" consists mainly of the following blocks, which is shown Fig.3.1.

- Microcontroller
- Microwave Doppler Radar Sensor
- PIR Sensor
- Bomb Sensor
- Gas Sensor
- LCD
- ESP8266 Wi-Fi Module

3.2.1. Microcontroller

Microcontroller unit is the heart of the system, it is an integrated chip designed for performing a specific task or multifunction in an embedded system. PIC16F877A microcontroller is used here for sensing the input parameters and it is interfaced with the output parameter. It comprises the following features:

- High-Performance RISC CPU
- Operates at a speed of 20 MHz with 200 ns instruction cycle
- Operating voltage lies between 4.0V to 5.5V
- The industrial temperature range is from -450 to +850
- 15 Interrupt Sources and 35 single-word instructions are available in PIC microcontroller.
- Except for program branches, all others are single cycle instructions, program branches have two-cycle instructions.
- Flash Memory is 14.3 Kbytes the controller can process on 8192 words.

- Data SRAM and Data EEPROM are 368 bytes and 256 bytes respectively.
- Self-reprogrammable under software control
- In-Circuit Serial Programming can be done through two pins of 5v
- Watchdog Timer with on-chip RC oscillator
- Programmable code protection
- Power-saving Sleep mode
- Selectable oscillator options
- In-Circuit Debug via two pins

Peripheral Features
- It is made up of 33 I/O pins and 5 I/O ports.
- Timer0: 8-bit timer/counter with 8-bit prescaler
- Timer1: 16-bit timer/counter with prescaler
- Timer2: 8-bit timer/counter with 8-bit period register
- Two Capture, Compare, PWM modules
- 16-bit Capture input; max resolution 12.5 ns
- 16-bit Compare; max resolution 200 ns
- 10-bit PWM
- Synchronous Serial Port with two modes:
- SPI Master
- I2C Master and Slave
- USART/SCI with 9-bit address detection
- Parallel Slave Port (PSP)
- 8 bits wide with external RD, WR and CS controls
- Brown-out detection circuitry for Brown-Out Reset
- 10-bit, 8-channel A/D Converter
- Brown-Out Reset
- Analog Comparator module
- 2 analog comparators
- Programmable on-chip voltage reference module
- Programmable input multiplexing from device inputs and internal VREF
- Comparator outputs are externally accessible

3.2.2. PIR Sensor

PIR stands for Passive Infrared or Pyroelectric Infrared. PIR sensors are used for sensing the thermal radiations emitted from the body of humans when they are in motion. The warm-body motion is deducted as the target surface will have a change in temperature when compared with the outer atmosphere. This temperature change of the moving object i.e., humans may vary as higher value or lower value when compared with the outer ambient temperature.

The change in temperature depends upon the size of the target and the distance at which it is placed from the sensor. These movements are sensed by the PIR sensor. The output of the PIR sensor is in a logical manner (i.e.) 0 and 1. The logic signal is given to the transistor and then passes it to the PIC microcontroller.

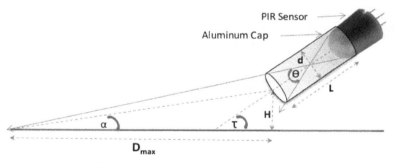

Fig.3.2. Cover Angle of the PIR Sensor

The coverage area and the detection range of the PIR sensor are incompatible with each other. To avoid that the following procedure was performed to obtain a unified coverage based on the parameters shown in Fig.3.2.

1) The top of the PIR sensor is mounted with an aluminum cap for reducing the coverage angle it makes on the target object. The length of the cap (L) was determined by relating it to the diameter of the lens which has a value of d=9.5mm. The calculations are made as follows:

$$\tan\left(\frac{\theta}{2}\right) = \frac{d}{L}$$

$$L = \frac{9.5mm}{\tan(30°)} = 16.5mm$$

2) The detecting range of the PIR sensor is set at an angle with a calculated degree value. The top of the sensor is tilted in such a way that the detection range is reduced to 2m. Assuming the height of the sensor as 0.5m from the ground level the tilting angle τ is given as follows:

$$\alpha = \tan^{-1}\left(\frac{H}{D_{max}}\right) = \tan^{-1}\left(\frac{0.5m}{2m}\right) = 14°$$

$$\tau = \frac{\theta}{2} + \alpha = \frac{60°}{2} + 14° = 44°$$

3.2.3. Microwave Doppler radar Sensor

Doppler microwave sensor HB100 is used for detecting the heartbeat signal by calculating the apparent change in the movement of signals between the transmitter and the receiver. The sensor has a bi-static Doppler transceiver radar module that sends a continuous wave signal to the target. Human beings trapped under the rubble are kept as a target; a signal with some amount of baseband signal has reflected the source. This signal denotes the heartbeat of trapped humans. A continuous-wave pulse is sent through the rubble of building and this wave has a higher coverage area than the PIR sensor.

Based upon the Doppler principle the frequency shift due to the motion of the target object is observed using this sensor. The frequency changes when the wave detects a moving object and then the device gets initiated. Microwave sensors could generate a false alarm as the wave from this module through the walls which can cause false indication.

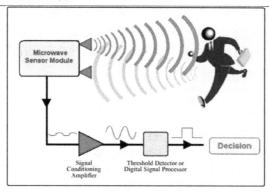

Fig.3.3. Working of Microwave Motion Sensor

A signal conditioning unit is used for manipulating the signals in such a way that it meets the requirements of the next stage for further processing. The SCU includes amplification, filtering, converting, range matching, isolation and any other processes required to make sensor output suitable for processing after conditioning as shown in Fig.3.3.

The sensor has three pins +5V, Out and GND. When a supply of +5V is given to the sensor it will generate output analog voltage in the range of 0V to 5V. This output can be read in a microcontroller through internal ADC (Analog to Digital Conversion) and is processed for further actions. It is suitable for false alarms reduction when works together with a passive infrared sensor.

3.2.4. Metal Bomb Sensor

Explosive bombs are detected by using a metal sensor, it an electronic device used for detecting the presence of nearby metal. A metal or bomb explosive buried underground or hidden inside an object can be detected using a metal bomb sensor. The metal detector works by electromagnetic field from the search coil of the detector to the surface of the earth. The metal hidden will generate an electromagnetic field of its own as the electromagnetic field of strengthens.

A signal response of the metal will be generated when the search coil of the detector receives a retransmitted signal. The output of the metal detector is fed to the microcontroller section for further processing.

3.2.5. Gas Sensor

Toxic gases present at the place of disaster are detected by using the MQ series of gas sensors. MQ series of sensors have a small heater molded inside an electrochemical sensor. Any hazardous gas leakage in the workplace, home or industry can be detected using this sensor. Sensors become sensitive for gases like LPG, i-butane, propane, methane, and hydrogen. The output of the signal is analog which can be read by the analog input of PIC microcontroller. Here MQ-2 gas sensor module is used for detecting the gas leakage in disaster areas.

Various gas sensors are available which may be used depending upon the type of gas leakage either it can be a natural gas leakage or other chemical leaks. The level of risk can be determined by the type of gas leakage and a sensor for that situation.

3.2.6.   LCD

16x2 LCD is used here to display the measurements of the victim detected. Also, the conditions of heartbeat, gas leakage and presence of metal data are displayed as per requirement. 16x2 LCD Module has 16 characters by 2 lines LCD Alphanumeric Display, built-in with the ST7066 controller. It operates at 5V power supply and it can be connected with a microcontroller in a 4/8-bit parallel interface.

3.2.7.   ESP 8266 Wi-Fi Module

The data received by the PIC microcontroller is transmitted for a wide range of communication using the ESP 8266 Wi-Fi module.

This Wi-Fi module is a complete package of the system on chip and microcontroller unit. It has an integrated TCP/IP protocol that allows any microcontroller to create internet access. This module is programmed using AT commands. The communication between the PIC and ESP 8266 is done using USART communication. For this serial transmission of data, the Wi-Fi module has a special library that checks each and every AT commands and then establishes a communication between the microcontroller and the Wi-Fi module.

3.3. CIRCUIT DIAGRAM

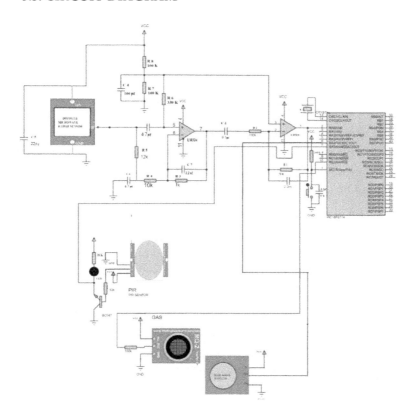

Fig.3.4. Circuit Diagram for Sensing Input Parameters

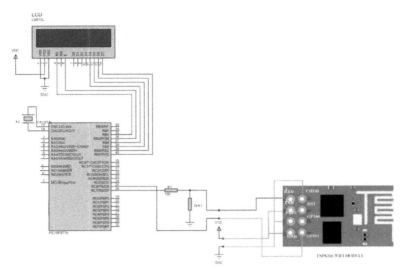

Fig.3.5. Circuit Diagram to Interface LCD and Wi-Fi Module with MCU

3.4. CIRCUIT DESCRIPTION

This project presents the system for alive human detection in a collapsed building and it checks for the presence of bombs and hazardous gas in the place. The various sensing units and the output units are interfaced with the various I/O lines of the controller. The circuit diagrams of the system are shown in Fig.3.4 and Fig.3.5. As per the user code, the controller controls the output unit with respect to the sensing unit output. The sensed data are collected and transmitted to the Internet through a Wi-Fi Module. 20 MHz crystal oscillator is used in the controller.

Port A of the microcontroller is fed as input to the PIR sensor, Microwave Doppler sensor, and metal sensor. The output of the Microwave sensor is connected to an operational amplifier that performs signal conditioning of the circuit and then it is connected to the PIC microcontroller. Port E of the microcontroller is taken as the input of the gas sensor. Port B is of the microcontroller is connected to the LCD display output for displaying the parameters.

Port C is used as an output for the Wi-Fi module. The microwave Doppler radar sensor HB100 is a miniature microwave sensor which works on the principle of Doppler shift. It passes microwaves through the rubble to detect the vital signs of life. Microwave reflects from humans; these signals are transmitted to a signal conditioning circuit. The signal conditioning circuit gets input signals from the analog sensors and gives a conditioned output of 0-5V DC.

The PIR sensor is used which is connected to RA5 of PIC16F877A microcontroller. The PIR sensor is used to detect the existence of living humans in disaster scenarios. This sensor does not emit any rays from it, it just absorbs the radiations generated by the hot bodies since the living body is composed of 96 degrees it absorbs the radiation once it detects it sends data to controller through PORTA then controller automatically gives display that the person is alive.

The signals from the sensors may be feeble, so a set of amplifiers are used to amplify the signals and are then sent to the controller for further decision making. The analog signal from the sensors is converted into a digital signal by PIC16F877A. The microcontroller gets the input from the sensor and converts analog to a digital signal by use of an internal ADC.

Many experiments were conducted to evaluate the performance of the system. The results of the experiments demonstrated that the system has the potential to achieve high performance in detecting living humans in obstructed environments relatively quickly and cost-effectively. 79% to 91% of detection accuracy was observed on the system depending on several factors such as the body position of the victim under the rubble, the variations in thermal radiations and light intensity of place of disaster, and by analyzing the parameters matching between the victim and the outer atmosphere.

PIR sensor along with the microwave Doppler is used for false alarms reduction. PIR detects the presence of a human, and with the help of a microwave motion sensor, the frequency of heartbeat and respiration rate can be measured. For ensuring the safety of people who are involved in rescue operation a bomb sensor (Metal Detector) and a gas sensor (MQ2) are interfaced with the microcontroller. The controller continuously monitors the parameter readings and will be displayed on the LCD. The data are also transmitted to the ESP8266 Wi-Fi module. It contains a self-calibrated RF allowing it to work under all operating conditions and requires no external RF parts.

3.5. PCB DESIGN

The materials required for the making of PCB are a copper clad sheet, a little point drilling machine, and ferric chloride. The main methods for preparing the PCB are:

3.5.1. Preparing Track Layout

The layout of the circuits is prepared using the PCB wizard software which is shown in Fig.3.6 and Fig.3.7. After drawing the circuit, it should be auto routed. This makes the PCB more economical and compact. The layout is printed on a white paper.

3.5.2. Transferring the Layout to the Copper Sheet

The layout printed on the white paper is printed on the copper clad sheet. The layout can also be redrawn on the copper-clad using paint or varnish. The schematic is transformed into the working films. The circuit is repeated conveniently to accommodate economically as many circuits as possible in a panel, which can be operated in every sequence of subsequent steps in the PCB process. This is called as Penalization.

3.5.3. Etching

It is the process of removing the unwanted copper from copper-clad where ever it is not required. Ferric chloride solution is popularly used for etching. This is made into a solution using water and kept it in a plastic tray. Immerse it for 2 hours. Keep stirring the solution to avoid sedimentation.

3.5.4. Drilling

The holes are made by a drilling machine for insertion of components. The drill bits made of solid coated tungsten carbide. Very small holes are drilled with high-speed drilling machines. These holes are called micro vias and their diameters are as small as 10 micrometers. The conductive holes are intended for the insertion of through-hole-component leads.

3.5.5. Soldering

It is the process of joining a metal sheet with an alloy whose melting point is less than that of materials that to be soldered. The alloy used for joining the metal is called solder.

3.6. PCB LAYOUT

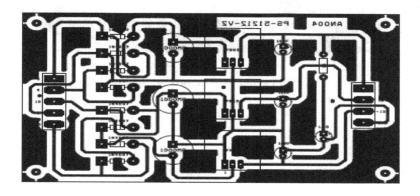

Fig.3.6. PCB Layout for the Power Supply

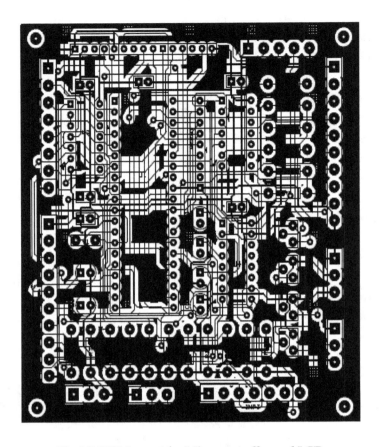

Fig.3.7. PCB Layout for Microcontroller and LCD

CHAPTER - 4

HARDWARE MODULES

4.1. POWER SUPPLY MODULE

All electronic circuits work only with a small D.C. voltage. Therefore a power supply unit is needed to provide the appropriate voltage supply to the circuits. The power supply unit consists of a transformer, rectifier, filter, and regulator (Fig.4.1). The main AC voltage is connected to the transformer which steps that AC voltage down to the level to the desired AC voltage.

Fig.4.1.   Functional Diagram of Power Supply

A diode rectifies AC voltage into a full-wave voltage that is initially filtered by a capacitor filter to produce a DC voltage. This resulting DC voltage usually has some ripple that not only has much less ripple voltage but also remains the same DC value even the DC voltage varies somewhat or the load connected to the output. The main things used in the power supply unit are Transformer, Rectifier, Filter, and Regulator. The 230V AV supply is converted into a 12V AC supply through the transformer.

The output of the transformer has the same frequency as in the input AC power. Here the bridge rectifier is used to convert the AC supply to the DC supply. This converted DC power supply has the ripple content and for the normal circuit operation, the ripple content of the DC power supply should be as low as possible. Because the ripple content of the power supply will reduce the life of the circuit. To reduce the ripple content in the DC power supply, the filter is used. The filter is nothing but the large value capacitance. The output waveform of the filter capacitance will almost be the straight line.

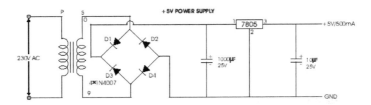

Fig.4.2. 5V Power Supply Circuit

This filtered output is not the regulated voltage. Especially the microcontroller-based circuit needs stable regulated 5V or 3.3V DC voltage to avoid the malfunction in MCUs. For this purpose, the 78xx regulator should be used in the circuit and it is shown in Fig.4.2. The xx represents the output stable voltage. If it is 7805, it produces 5V DC output and if it is 7812, it produces 12V DC output.

4.2. LIQUID CRYSTAL DISPLAY MODULE

Liquid crystal display (LCD) is a flat electronic panel or an electronic display. The LCD module is used here for displaying the values of parameters read by the PIC microcontroller. In recent years the LCD is finding widespread use replacing seven-segment LEDs.

- The LCD can display numbers, characters, and graphical symbols.
- The LCD is more energy-efficient than CRT.

- In LCD, the graphics and characters can be programmed easily.

The following steps has to be taken while interfacing LCD with PIC16F877A,

Step 1:

Determine the type of LCD which is specified as 16x1, 16x2, and 20x2 in the format AxB where A is the number of columns and B is the number of rows.

Step 2:

Identify the pin functions; most of the LCD's follow the standard Hitachi pinout.

Step 3:

Connect the pins RS, RW, E, D0 - D7 to port pins on the microcontroller. Data bus pins are connected with upper port B (4-bit mode) and the RS, E pins are connected with lower port B.

LCD Commands

Table 4.2.1 LCD Commands

No	HEX Value	COMMAND TO LCD
1	0x01	Clear Display Screen
2	0x30	Function Set: 8-bit, 1 Line, 5x7 Dots
3	0x38	Function Set: 8-bit, 2 Line, 5x7 Dots
4	0x20	Function Set: 4-bit, 1 Line, 5x7 Dots
5	0x28	Function Set: 4-bit, 2 Line, 5x7 Dots
6	0x06	Entry Mode
7	0x08	Display off, Cursor off
8	0x0E	Display on, Cursor on
9	0x0C	Display on, Cursor off
10	0x0F	Display on, Cursor blinking
11	0x18	Shift entire display left
12	0x1C	Shift entire display right
13	0x10	Move cursor left by one character
14	0x14	Move cursor right by one character
15	0x80	Force cursor to beginning of 1st row
16	0xC0	Force cursor to beginning of 2nd row

These are all the LCD commands. Based on the task in hand, the user needs to give the command to LCD. Based on the commands given by the user the LCD can be controlled.

Pin specifications of LCD are listed below:

- VCC, VSS, and VEE
  - Provide +5V and ground to the VCC and VSS, respectively and VEE is used for controlling LCD screen contrast.
- RS - Register Select
  - There are two important registers inside the LCD. The RS pin is used for their selection as follows.
  - If RS=0, it selects the command register to allow the user to send a command such as clear display, cursor at home, etc.
  - If RS=1, the data register is selected, it allows the user to send the data to be displayed to the LCD.
- R/W - Read/Write
  - The R/W pin is used to identify the read and write operations of LCD. If R/W=1, it performs the reading operation or if R/W=0, it performs the writing operation.
- E - Enable
  - The enable pin is used by the LCD to latch information presented to its data pins. When data is supplied to data pins, a high-to-low pulse must be applied to this pin for the LCD to latch in the data present at the data pins. This pulse must be a minimum of 450ns wide.
- D0-D7
  - The D0 – D7 are a data pin, used to send the data to LCD through the internal register. To display letters and numbers, we send ASCII codes for the letters A-Z, a-z, and numbers 0-9 to these pins while making RS=1.

Table 4.2.2 Symbol and Functions of LCD

Pin	Symbol	Function
1	V_{SS}	Ground
2	V_{DD}	Supply Voltage
3	V_0	Contrast Setting
4	RS	Register Select
5	R/W	Read/Write Select
6	En	Chip Enable Signal
7-14	DB0-DB7	Data Lines
15	A/V_{EE}	Ground for the backlight
16	K	V_{CC} for backlight

The ENABLE pin is used to latch the data present on the data pins (Fig.4.3). A High-Low signal is required to latch the data. The LCD interprets and executes our command at the instant the EN line is brought low.

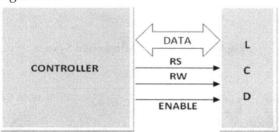

Fig.4.3. LCD Interfaced with Microcontroller

4.2.1. Advantages

- Very compact and light
- Low power consumption
- No geometric distortion
- Little or no flicker depending on backlight technology
- Not affected by screen burn-in
- No high voltage or other hazards present during repair/service
- Can be made in almost any size or shape

4.3. MICROWAVE DOPPLER RADAR SENSOR MODULE

The principle of detection is done by sending microwave signals of X-band frequency through the rubble to detect vital signs of life. Microwave beams will reflect from some objects which includes humans (Fig.4.4). When the microwave beam hits the body, the signal is reflected with an additional modulation created by movements of heart and lungs. The received modulated signals show the presence of alive human inside the rubble.

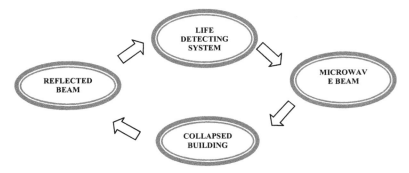

Fig.4.4. Principle of Microwave System

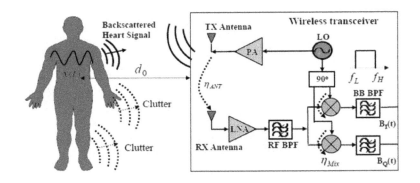

Fig.4.5. Microwave Sensor to Detect Heart Signals

With the modulated signal there are some signals, which are reflected from the immobile object such as rubble or debris.

The wave reflected from the rubble or the surface of the ground is cancelled as thoroughly as possible. The principle of human detection is done primarily by sending 10 GHz microwave frequency electromagnetic signal from the oscillator and it is passed through rubble to detect vital signs of life. The microwave has the property to penetrate through barriers and will reflect from some objects. The reception of signals shows the presence of alive human under the rubble.

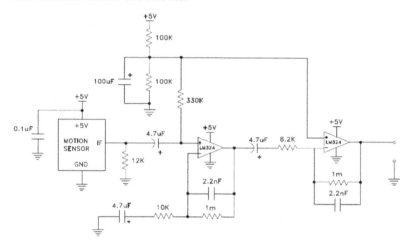

Fig.4.6. Preamplifier Circuit for Microwave Sensor

An antenna is taken as reference and from that antenna a signal with known frequency is transmitted to another receiving antenna placed at the receiver (Fig.4.5). The receiver receives the signal from the transmitter and reflects it to the transmitting antenna for the measurement of Doppler shift signal. The basic formulas used for denoting the received frequency is given by:

$$f_r = f_0 \left(\frac{v \pm v_0}{v \pm v_s} \right)$$

Here fr is the received frequency, fo the source, vs relative speed of the source, vo the observer speed, and v the speed of the waves in the medium.

While doing practical calculations the difference in frequency is taken into consideration and the change in frequency is given by:

$$\Delta f = f_r - f_0$$

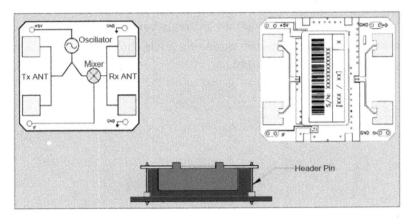

Fig.4.7. Structure of HB100 Microwave Doppler radar Sensor

The block diagram of HB100 sensor has an oscillator that produces a transmitting frequency and a mixer is in-built to analyze the difference between the transmitted and received signals (Fig.4.7). The oscillator sends a wave of frequency 10 GHz. When no object is found at the receiver then the output signal becomes zero. A variation in output signal is obtained when a moving object is found at the receiving part.

A Doppler module has an inbuilt oscillator which is responsible for generating the transmitting frequency. This frequency when mixes with the receiving signal a sinusoidal output is produced. This output is derived by the change in frequency. The sinusoidal output can be read by the microcontroller. HB100 Miniature Microwave Motion Sensor is an X-Band Bi-Static Doppler transceiver module. It has a built-in Dielectric Resonator Oscillator (DRO) and a pair of Micro-strip patch antenna array, making it ideal for usage in motion detection equipment. The module operates at +5V DC for Continuous wave (CW) operation.

The detecting range of sensor module depends upon the size of the target on which the signal is transmitted. The reflectivity of the signal to noise ratio also makes a variation in the detection. The sensor is placed in such a way that the antenna faces the target object. The physical structure of a HB100 microwave Doppler module is shown in Fig 4.8.

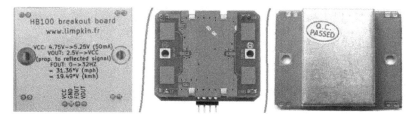

Fig.4.8. HB100 Microwave Doppler radar Sensor Module

4.3.1. HB100 Features

- It has a low power consumption of 30 mA
- The signals are operated in continuous wave and a flat profile of the sensor makes it easy for use.
- It has a long detection range approximately 20 meters.
- Supply voltage between 4.75V and 5.25V
- X-Band frequency: 10.525 GHz
- Minimum Power Output: 13 dBm EIRP

4.4. PASSIVE INFRA-RED SENSOR MODULE

Human beings emit a radiation which is produced due to the temperature of the body. This radiation is known as Infra-red radiation. It is also called as thermal radiation as the body temperature of humans or any other object produces this radiation. These Infra-red radiations are invisible to human eye but they can be detected by using electronic devices. The electronic device used for sensing Infra-red radiation is Passive Infra-red sensor which is also called as Pyroelectric sensor. These sensors measures the amount of IR radiated from the target object.

This is used for detecting the presence of human and the movement of human body creates a difference in the radiation emitted from their body. This change is identified by the PIR sensor. The name Passive is given as the sensor does not emit any infra-red radiation but it passively senses the radiation emitted from the target object (Fig.4.9). Pyroelectric devices are made up of crystalline material when exposed to infrared radiation generates an electric charge.

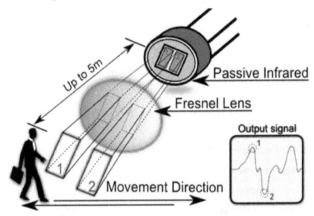

Fig.4.9. PIR-Theory of Operation

The value of voltage varies according to the amount of infrared striking the element. The varying voltage is measured by an on-board amplifier. A special filter called Fresnel lens is present for focusing the infrared signals onto the element.

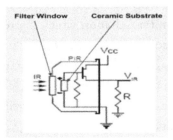

Fig.4.10. PIR-Structural Description

As the infrared signals change rapidly, the on-board amplifier trips the output to indicate motion (Fig.4.10).

The detected radiations are converted into an electrical charge, which is proportional to the detected level of the radiation. The detected radiations are converted into an electrical charge, which is proportional to the detected level of the radiation. For further improvement of the signal the sensor has an in built FET that feds the incoming radiation as output signal to the output pin. The PIR sensor detects the presence up to 10 meters.

The core of a PIR sensor is made from an average of 1/4 inch square of natural or artificial pyroelectric materials, usually in the form of a thin film or out of Gallium Nitride (GaN), Caesium Nitrate(CsNO3), polyvinyl fluorides, and derivatives of Phenylpyrazine. The IR radiations are passed on to the PIR sensor using the front surface of the sensor. The sensors can be made as a separate integrated part or it can be manufactured with one, two or four pixels of pyroelectric materials built on its surface.

The amount of thermal radiations from the movement of victim produces a corresponding value of the electric charge. The thermal radiations may also include the outer atmosphere radiations present around the victim. To cancel this signal and also to avoid false alarm indication the pair of sensors pixels can be wired as opposite inputs and fed to a differential amplifier.

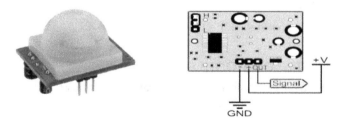

Fig.4.11. PIN OUT of PIR Sensor Module

The disturbances of light or thermal radiations for a larger amount of time if continuous signals are passing on to the sensor it may further damage the working of sensor therefore cancelling of the outer thermal radiation is an important scenario which is done by the differential amplifier.

The damage caused due to the outer thermal radiations stop the sensor from further processing. This PIR Sensor detects motion by measuring changes in the infrared (heat) levels emitted by surrounding objects. This motion can be detected by checking for a sudden change in the surrounding IR patterns. When motion is detected, the PIR sensor outputs a high signal on its output pin (Fig.4.11). This logic signal can be read by a microcontroller and it can indicate that a person is detected at a particular area.

Table 4.4.1 Pin Configuration of PIR Sensor

Pin	Name	Function
-	GND	Ground: 0V
+	Vin	3.3 to 5V DC
Out	Output	Connected to I/O pin

4.4.1. Features

Detection range up to 20 feet away with reduced false alarm indication. Product size makes it easy to conceal compatible with many other microcontrollers.

- Power requirements: 3.3 to 5 VDC; >3 mA
- Communication: Single bit high/low output
- Operating temperature: 32 to 122 °F (0 to 50 °C)
- Dimensions: 1.27 x 0.96 x 1.0 in (32.2 x 24.3 x 25.4 mm)

4.5. GAS SENSOR MODULE

Industrial explosions or some gas leakage accidents can also cause damage to human life. A massive industrial explosion can have some leakage of hazardous gases, and that may explode during the rescue operation. For creating prevention during this scenario the sensitive gases are sensed by the MQ-2 gas sensor primarily made up of SnO_2 that offers a lower conductivity in clean air. The concentration of gas sensed by the sensor increases once it identifies a combustible gas in the same way the conductivity of the sensor also increases.

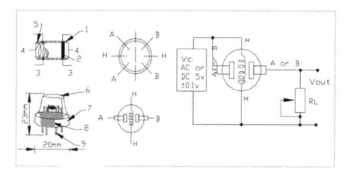

Fig.4.12. Structural Description of MQ2 Sensor

The change of conductivity is converted into a corresponding output signal of gas concentration. MQ-2 gas sensor has a high level of sensitivity to gases like LPG, Propane, methane, etc. This makes it suitable for every application.

The sensor has 6 pins; 3 pins connected in the upper surface and 3 pins connected in the lower surface as shown in Fig 4.12. The pins denoting A and B are the terminals of the sensor and H is the heating element placed between the electrochemical sensors. The electrodes are fabricated by mounting a high surface area precious metal on the porous hydrophobic membrane. The working electrode contacts with both the electrolyte and the air are monitored through a porous membrane. The electrolyte most commonly used is a mineral acid the electrodes and housing are usually in a plastic which contains a gas entry hole for the gas and electrical contacts.

The sensor is made up of a porous membrane that senses the incoming gas diffusing through the surface. The sensed gas is passed on to the electrode inside for further process of oxidation and reduction. This reaction is an electrochemical process that results in creating a corresponding output voltage in the external circuit. The circuitry connections of this sensor are made in such a way that a variable resistor is connected in series with the sensor to form a voltage dividing circuit.

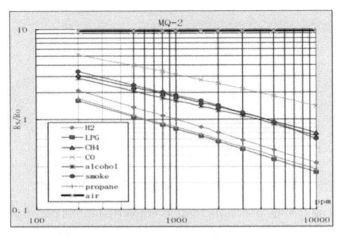

Fig.4.13. Characteristic Curve Showing Sensitivity of Different Gases

The heating element gets heated as it senses the presence of gas in the atmosphere. This change in heat is converted into a change in the value of resistance from which an output voltage is generated with the help of the voltage divider circuit. By connecting an ADC the values are fed into the microcontroller.

The sensitivity level of the sensor varies depending upon the gas it senses. The sensitivity characteristic curve for different gases is shown below in Fig 4.13.

4.5.1. Character Configuration of MQ 2 sensors

- Power supply Voltage : 5 volts
- Output voltage Range : 0-0.9 Volts.
- Good sensitivity to Combustible gas in wide range
- High sensitivity to LPG, Propane and Methane
- Long life and low cost and simple driver circuit

4.6. METAL BOMB SENSOR MODULE

A metal sensor module is used for detecting the presence of explosive metal during the rescue operation. It works on the principle of Electromagnetic induction.

The search coil present in the module emits an alternating current with the help of an oscillator in the circuit (Fig.4.14). The coil strengthens the magnetic field in that area by detecting a metal object. Due to this strong magnetic field, the metal object is hidden under the ground surface or a collapsed building an eddy current is produced. This leads to the production of the magnetic field retransmitted to the search coil. The retransmitted signal shows the presence of metal objects.

Fig.4.14. Metal Bomb Sensor Module

The metal sensor module used in this system produces a DC output for the corresponding input it receives from the metallic object. It has an inbuilt miniature metallic circuit as shown in fig 4.15 and a search coil placed in a small sensor module. This dimension of the sensor makes it easier to use in many applications as they are compact and easily portable. It detects metal objects up to 7 cm and giving active low output with LED and buzzer indication.

4.6.1. Features

- Detection range adjustable up to 7 cm
- Operation range varies according to size of the metallic object
- Power Supply: 5V DC and 50 mA max
- Detection Indicators: LED and Buzzer
- Digital output: Active with logic '0'
- Dimensions : 52x71 mm

The heart of this sensor is the inductive oscillator circuit which monitors high-frequency current loss in a coil. The circuit is designed for any metallic body detection by detecting the variations in the high-frequency eddy current losses. The output signal level is altered by an approaching metallic object. The output signal from the sensor depends upon the change in the value of the supply current. Depending upon the distance at which the metallic object is present from the sensor there is a change in the supply current independent of the supply voltage.

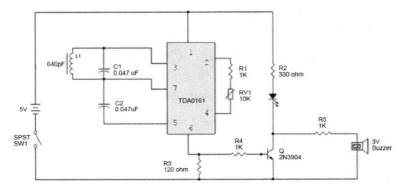

Fig.4.15. Metal Detector Circuit

The output current value is high if the distance between the metallic object and the sensor is very less. There is a dense magnetic field it increases the output current. In the same way, the output current is low when the metal is identified at a longer distance from the sensor.

4.7. ESP 8266 Wi-Fi MODULE

The purpose of the Internet of Things is whatever work we do has to be connected with the Internet as it can be accessed by anyone around the world. In this system, the data acquired by the microcontroller is transmitted for a wide range of communication using a Wi-Fi module ESP 8266. This module can be either used separately for creating network access or it can be connected with a microcontroller for establishing internet access. It has a TCP/IP protocol responsible for internet access.

This module can be used with many applications as it has an integrated cache memory. It has an ultra low power, 32-bit microcontroller unit, with the 16-bit short mode, clock speed support 80/160 MHz, supports the RTOS, includes Wi-Fi MAC/BB/RF/PA/LNA, and onboard antenna. Due to the self-contained package, it can act as a separate Wi-Fi adaptor and wireless internet access can be added to any microcontroller unit for performing a communication task. A special library function is used for checking the AT commands transferred between the microcontroller and ESP module. This library function checks every command before they are transmitting or receiving the data.

Fig 4.16. ESP 8266 Wi-Fi Module

The compact PCB design of the ESP module (Fig.4.16) and its small dimension with a low cost is the reason it is used for many IoT applications. Most of the IoT application uses this module as it produces a great range of communication. The Tx/Rx pin present in this module transmits and receives the Ethernet buffer to and fro the controller and the Wi-Fi module. An advantage to the microcontroller is only less external circuitry needed as the external connections are made using USART communication.

The commands and data are serially transmitted with this communication. There is no need for a TCP/IP stack running in the microcontroller separately the protocol present in the module is enough for network access. The addressable capability of this module with USART creates an extreme demand for IoT applications. ESP 8266 has powerful on-board processing and storage capabilities.

The high degree of on-chip integration allows for minimal external circuitry, and the entire solution, including the front-end module, is designed to occupy minimal PCB area. The microcontroller can be connected to this module and data can be pushed to the internet. Using this module a link can be created through which the process taking place in the disaster area can be monitored and anyone can have access to the ongoing process. A database can also be stored about the details of people saved in the rescue operations.

Table 4.7.1 Pin Description of ESP 8266 Wi-Fi Module

Name	Type	Description
VCC	-	Voltage DC input 3.3V
RST	-	Reset
CH-PD	Chip Enable	High: On, Chip works properly Low: Off, Small current
TXD	Output	Serial Port Transmit Data (TTL)
GND	-	Ground
GPIO 2		UART Tx during flash programming
GPIO 0		SPICS 2
RXD	Input	Serial port receive data (TTL)

4.7.1 Features
- Serial UART Interface
- 802.11 BGN
- Wi-Fi Direct
- Built-in TCP/IP
- Efficient and perfect AT commands
- AP, STA , AP+STA modes supported
- Onboard PCB Antenna for transmitting and receiving the data

4.7.2 Specifications
- Simple set of AT commands

- Controlled via USART interface at 115200 baud rate
- No additional circuits other than TXD/RXD in microcontroller needed
- Support three modes of protocol
- Integrated TCP/IP protocol stack
- Integrated TR switch, LNA, power amplifier and matching network
- Requires 19.5 dBm output power
- Less than 10 micro amperes output power

CHAPTER – 5

SOFTWARE IMPLEMENTATION

5.1. MPLAB IDE

MPLAB IDE is easy to learn and use the Integrated Development Environment (IDE). The IDE provides a firmware development platform to develop and debug firmware for Microchip's PIC microcontroller families. MPLAB IDE can compile and simulate many languages like Assembly Language, C language (HIGH-TECH C, PIC C, WIN C are all versions) and some other languages. MPLAB has a user-friendly environment that helps the programmer to create and debug any complex programs.

MPLAB IDE provides functions that allow programs to

- Create and edit source files of any mentioned language
- Group dislocated files into projects accordingly
- Debug and modify source code
- Simulate and view the results immediately in steps
- Debug executable logic using simulator or emulator
- Creates HEX files used to program PIC using any programmer

A variety of windows allows the programmer to view the contents of all data and program memory locations virtually. This helps the programmer to use memory efficiently.

The source code, program memory, and absolute listing windows allow the programmer to view the source code and its assembly-level equivalent separately. MPLAB IDE comes with a variety of internal GUI functions such as MPASM assembler; MP LINK object linker and MPLAB object librarian also included with MPLAB IDE. MPLAB IDE also supports the MPLAB C17 and C18C compilers, MPLAB ICD 2000 in-circuit emulator, MPLAB ICD and MPLAB ICD 2 in-circuit debuggers, PIC START plus and PRO MATE II programmers and other third-party tools are also supported.

- It has up to four buffer level which can be used to compare different reads from IC which is used to debug and verify the download.
- It has a disassembly viewer that displays the assembly languages of the selected PIC from the HEX file itself.

5.2. PROTEUS 8 PROFESSIONAL

Proteus 8 is a single application with many service modules offering different functionality (schematic capture, PCB layout, etc.). The wrapper that enables all of the various tools to communicate with each other consists of three main parts.

Application Framework

Proteus 8 consists of a single application (PDS.EXE). This is the framework or container which hosts all of the functionality of Proteus. ISIS, ARES, 3DV all open as tabbed windows within this framework and therefore all have access to the common database.

Common Database

The common database contains information about parts used in the project. A part can contain both a schematic component and a PCB footprint as well as both user and system properties. Shared access to this database by all application modules makes possible a huge number of new features, many of which will evolve throughout the version 8 lifecycle.

Live Netlist

Together with the common database, the maintenance of a live netlist allows all open modules to automatically reflect changes. The most obvious example of this is wiring in ISIS producing rats nest connections in ARES but it goes much further than that. The new Bill of Materials module contains a live viewer and the 3D Viewer and Design Explorer are also linked into the live netlist.

In Proteus 8, the relationship between Schematic Design and PCB Layout involves a shared database and is far more integrated. We, therefore, have a single project file rather than separate design and layout files. We can create a new project or import a legacy schematic/layout via the options on the home page.

Schematic

If you are creating a schematic check the box at the top of the screen and then select the template on which you want to base the schematic. Those provided by Lab center contain different sizes of the work area, although you can customize and save your templates from within the schematic capture module.

PCB Layout

If you are creating a PCB check the box at the top of the screen and select from the available templates. PCB templates contain pre-defined board edges; mounting holes and a full set of technical data (design rules, layers in use, default units, etc.). As with schematic, you can customize and save your templates from within the PCB layout module.

Firmware

If you are creating an embedded design and want to simulate your firmware, check the create firmware box at the top of the screen and then select your controller and compiler using the combo boxes. If selected, the quick start files checkbox will generate a skeleton firmware project for you and configure project settings for compilation.

5.3. FLOW CHART

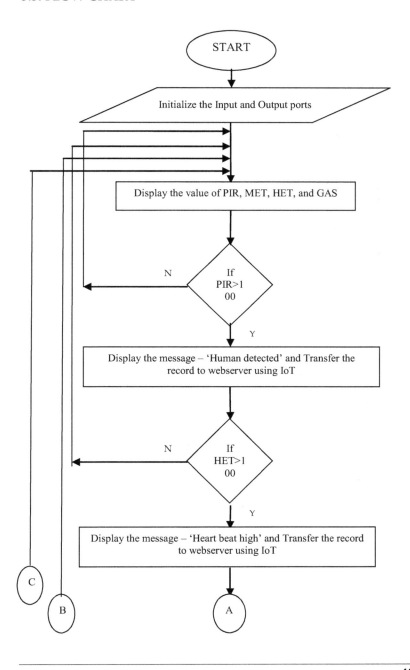

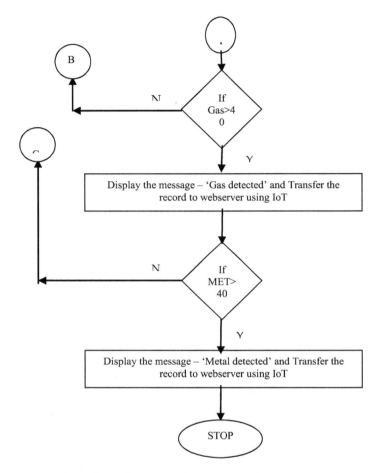

Fig. 5.1. Flow chart of IoT Based System for the Detection of Trapped Victims in Disaster Scenarios

5.4. SOURCE CODE

//* Main program *//

```
#include<htc.h>
#include<math.h>
#include "4bit.c"
#include "uart.c"
#include "pic16F877A.h"
void main()
{
// declaration and initialization of variables
unsigned int PIR,MET,GAS,HET;
unsigned char z;
TRISA0=1;                       // Initialize PORTA as input
TRISA1=1;
TRISA2=1;
TRISA3=1;
TRISD=0x00;                     // Initialize PORTD as output
TRISE=0;                        // Initialize PORTE as output
ADCON1=0x42;
pic_init();
lcd_init();                     // Initialize Lcd
uart_init();                    // Initialize UART
lcd_cmd(0x80);
string(" EMERGENCY ");          // EMERGENCY
lcd_cmd(0xC0);
string("RESCUE SYSTEM");        // RESCUE SYSTEM
delay(2000);
lcd_cmd(0x01);
while(1)
{
lcd_cmd(0x80);
string("PIR:");                 // PIR: is displayed
PIR=adc_init(0xc5);             //conversion of AD Value
```

```c
adc_conv(PIR,0x84);              // Digital value of PIR is
displayed
delay(1000);
lcd_cmd(0xc0);
string("MET:");                  // MET: is displayed
MET=adc_init(0xcd);              //conversion of AD value
adc_conv(MET,0xC4);              // Digital value of MET
delay(1000);
lcd_cmd(0x88);                   // GAS: is displayed
string("GAS:");
GAS=adc_init(0xdd);              //conversion of AD value
 adc_conv(GAS,0x8C);             // Digital value of GAS
delay(1000);
 lcd_cmd(0xc8);
string("HET:");                  // HET: is displayed
HET=adc_init(0xd5);              //conversion of AD value
adc_conv(HET,0xCC);              // Digital value of HET
delay(1000);
if(PIR>100)
{
RB0=0;
lcd_cmd(0xc0);
string("PERSON DETECTED");          // PERSON DETECTED
string_uart("PERSON DETECTED");     // Displayed message
tx(0x0d);tx(0x0a);
tx(0x0d);tx(0x0a);
delay(1000);
 lcd_cmd(0x01);
}
if(MET>40)
{
RB1=0;
lcd_cmd(0xc0);
 string("METAL DETECTED");          // METAL DETECTED
 string_uart("METAL DETECTED`");    // Displayed message
```

```
tx(0x0d);tx(0x0a);
tx(0x0d);tx(0x0a);
 delay(1000);
 lcd_cmd(0x01);
}
if(GAS>40)
{
RB2=0;
lcd_cmd(0xc0);
 string("GAS HIGH");              // GAS HIGH is displayed
string_uart("GAS HIGH");          // Displayed message
tx(0x0d);tx(0x0a);
tx(0x0d);tx(0x0a);
delay(1000);
 lcd_cmd(0x01);
}
if(HET>40)
{
RB2=0;
cd_cmd(0xc0);
string("HEART BEAT HIGH");        // HEART BEAT HIGH
 string_uart("HEART BEAT HIGH");  // Displayed message
tx(0x0d);tx(0x0a);
tx(0x0d);tx(0x0a);
 delay(1000);
 lcd_cmd(0x01);
}
}}
```

// * Sub program for LCD module connections * //
```
//#include<pic.h>
void pic_lcd_init();                // Initialize LCD display
void lcd_data(unsigned char d);
void lcd_cmd(unsigned char d);
```

```c
void lcd_init();
void delay(unsigned char x);
void adc_conv(unsigned char ,unsigned char );
unsigned int adc_init(unsigned char);
void string(const char *p);
void delay(unsigned char x)        // delay operation
{
        unsigned int i,j;
        for(i=0;i<x;i++)
        for(j=0;j<1275;j++);
}
void pic_lcd_init()
{
TRISD=0X0F;
PORTD=0X0F;                        // Initialize PORTD as input
PORTE=0X00;                        // Initialize PORTE as output
TRISE0=0;
TRISE1=0;
TRISE2=0;
}
void lcd_data(unsigned char d)  // Data to display
{
RE2=1;
RE1=0;    //rs
delay(2);
PORTD=d&0xF0;
RE0=1;
delay(2);
RE0=0;
PORTD=(d<<4)&0xF0;
RE0=1;
delay(2);
RE0=0;
}
void lcd_cmd(unsigned char d)
```

```
{
RE2=0;
RE1=0;
delay(2);
PORTD=d&0xF0;
RE0=1;
delay(2);
RE0=0;
PORTD=(d<<4)&0xF0;
RE0=1;
delay(2);
RE0=0;
}
void lcd_init()                    // Initialize LCD display
{
lcd_cmd(0x02);
lcd_cmd(0x28);
lcd_cmd(0x0e);
lcd_cmd(0x80);
}


// analog to digital operation
void adc_conv(unsigned char dat,unsigned char x)
{
unsigned char a,b,c;
a=dat/100;
b=(dat%100)/10;
c=dat%10;
lcd_cmd(x);
lcd_data(a+0x30);
lcd_data(b+0x30);
lcd_data(c+0x30);
}
unsigned int adc_init(unsigned char ch){
```

```
            unsigned char c;
            ADCON0=ch;
            //ADCON1=0x42;
            ADON=1;
            ADGO=1;
            while(ADGO==1);
            c=ADRESH*2;
            //adc_conv(c*1.96);
            return c;
}
```

// Operation for displaying string data

```
void string(const char *p)
{
while(*p)
{
lcd_data(*p++);
}}
```

// * Sub program for ADC *//

```
//#include<pic.h>
void pic_init();
void uart_init();
void tx(unsigned char);
void string(const char *q);
unsigned char rx();
void pic_init()
{
TRISC7=1;
TRISC6=0;
}
void uart_init()
{
TXSTA=0X20;              // Configure transmitter pin
RCSTA=0X90;              // Configure receiver pin
```

```
SPBRG=30;
}
void tx(unsigned char byte)
{
int i;
TXREG=byte;
while(!TXIF)
for(i=0;i<=400;i++);
}
unsigned char rx()
{
while(!RCIF);
return RCREG;
}
```

// Transfer and Receive string value

```
void string_uart(const char *q)
{
while(*q)
{
tx(*q++);
}}
```

// Analog to Digital process

```
void uart_conv(unsigned char dat)
{
unsigned char a,b,c;
a=dat/100;
b=(dat%100)/10;
c=dat%10;
tx(a+0x30);
tx(b+0x30);
tx(c+0x30);
}
```

CHAPTER - 6
SYSTEM TESTING

An IoT based system to detect trapped victims in disaster scenarios using Doppler microwave and passive infrared technology has been designed and tested successfully. It is very compatible to use. Once the system is energized the title will be displayed on the LCD display. The microcontroller will initialize the Wi-Fi Module.

All the sensors are connected to the PIC microcontroller. The microcontroller senses the data and passes it to the ESP 8266 Wi-Fi module. The PIR sensor senses the presence of humans within approximately 10 meters from the sensor. When the human is identified it is displayed on the LCD as HUMAN DETECTED.

The heartbeat frequencies are detected using a microwave Doppler radar sensor. 10 GHz signals are transmitted from the oscillator in the module. The movement of the human body under the rubbles causes the body to reflect back the signals.

These signals denote the presence of a heartbeat and it is displayed on the LCD as HEARTBEAT HIGH. A link is created using the Wi-Fi module to send the data sensed by the microcontroller module to the webserver page.

6.1 SIMULATION RESULTS
The system for detecting human presence using IoT is simulated using Proteus software.

The circuit model of the above system is shown and sensors are connected to measure the output.

A) Screen shot of web page

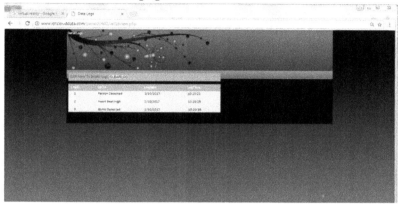

B) Normal condition

In normal conditions, all the sensor values will be less than the preset value.

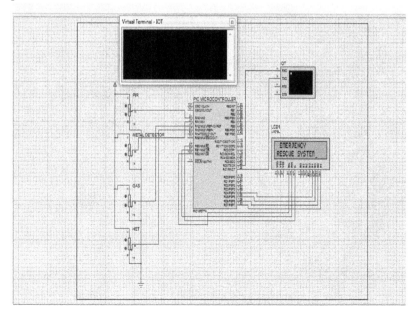

C) Sensors Initiated

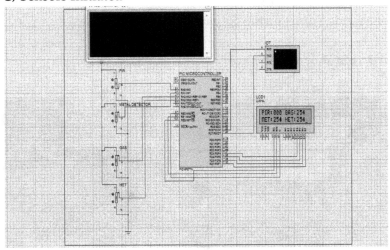

D) Human Detected

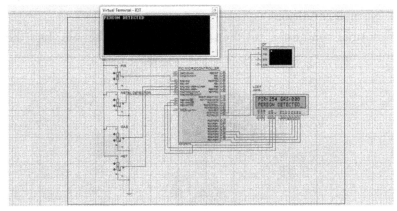

E) Human Detected and the Detected human is alive

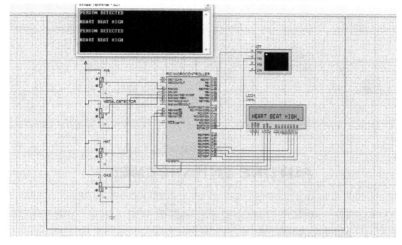

CHAPTER - 7
FUTURE ENHANCEMENT

- The system can be expanded with more number of parameters.
- This concept can be implemented in a Quad-Copter to find humans in a very short duration.
- A robot capable of carrying the victim to secure places can be designed.
- Proper lighting can be added for night time usage.
- Parameters to locate the location of disaster can be added.
- The wearable module of this can be made for people working in military, coal mine and rescue operations.
- Several people can be detected, an area with more number of people can be located and that area can be given first preference to save many lives.
- An emergency ambulance system for this module can be attached so that people can be rescued.
- It can be used in military applications, coal mine areas to ensure the safety of the people working at those places.

CHAPTER - 8

CONCLUSION

An IoT based system to detect the trapped victims in disaster scenarios using Doppler microwave and passive infrared technology gives a higher level of safety during the rescue operation of trapped victims. This sensor network assures in saving many lives in the place of disaster. The Wi-Fi module in this system provided a wide range of communication through which many people can get details regarding the detection of alive human beings in disasters in such calamity hit zones.

The proposed system is providing low-cost trapped-victim detection for rescue operations in extreme situations. This system has detected the heartbeat signals of trapped victims in rubble. The system runs with the PIR sensor hence it reduced the false alarm indication of human presence. The system is emerging and gaining high applications in the wide-area such as earthquake rescue, bomb blast hazardous, industrial explosions and military area. The system is equipped with a gas sensor and bomb sensor for detecting fire and metals in rescue scenarios respectively. A wireless communication link is used to communicate with the rescue team whenever a need arises.

The data can be used by the government authority regarding the rescue operation taking place at the place of disaster. The entire system uses an IoT platform as a back-end to push, record, publish and analyze sensed data. Hence this work had met its objective to perform effective detection and rescue during a disaster and fulfilled the goal of improving the society economically and technologically with a functional real-time project. This work could be considered as a reference to the researchers for real-time wireless body-to-body implementation using a dedicated protocol for the disaster relief context.

References

[1]   Binoy Shah and Howie Choset (2004). Survey on Urban Search and Rescue Robotics. Journal of the Robotics Society of Japan, 22(5), 582-586.

[2]   Rapee Krerngkamjornkit (2013). Human Body Detection in Search and Rescue Operation Conducted by Unmanned Aerial Vehicles. Advanced Materials Research, 655, 1077-1085.

[3]   Gao, Massey, Selavo, Crawford, Chen, Lorincz, Shnayder, Hauenstein, Dabiri, Jeng, et al. (2007). The advanced health and disaster aid network: A light-weight wireless medical system for triage. IEEE Trans. Biomed. Circuits Syst., 1, 203–216.

[4]   Negra, Jemili, Belghith (2016). Wireless Body Area Networks: Applications and Technologies. Procedia Comput. Sci., 83, 1274–1281.

[5]   Varun, Menon, Priya (2016). Ensuring Reliable Communication in Disaster Recovery Operations with Reliable Routing Technique. Mob. Inf. Syst., doi:10.1155/2016/9141329.

[6]   George S.M., Zhou, Chenji, Won M, Lee, Y.O, Pazarloglou, Stoleru, Barooah (2010). A wireless ad hoc and sensor network architecture for situation management in disaster response. IEEE Commun. Mag., 48, 128–136.

[7]   T. Miller, L. Potter, and J. McCorkle (1997). RFI suppression for ultra wideband radar. IEEE Trans. Aerosp. Electron. Syst., 33, 1142-1156.

[8]   U. Zakia, M. W. Turza, E. Karim, T. Z. Moumita and T. A. Khan (2016). A Navigation system for rescue operation during disaster management using LTE advanced network and WPAN. 2016 IEEE 7th Annual Information Technology, Electronics and Mobile Communication Conference (IEMCON), Vancouver, BC, pp.1-6. doi: 10.1109/IEMCON.2016.7746280.

[9]   M. Jelen, E. M. Bieble (2006). Multi-frequency sensor for remote measurement of breath and heart beat. Advances in Radio Sci., 4, 79-83.

[10] Nicholas Petrochilos, Meriam Rezk, Anders Host-Madsen, Victor Lubecke, Olga Boric-Ludecke (2007). Blind separation of human heartbeats and breathing by the use of a Doppler radar remote sensing. IEEE international conference on Acoustics Speech and Signal Processing ICASSP, 1, 333-336.

[11] M. Donelli (2011). A rescue radar system for the detection of victims trapped under rubble based on the independent component analysis algorithm. Progress In Electromagnetics Research M, 19, 173-181. DOI: 10.2528/PIERM11061206.

[12] Akiyama, I., N. Yoshizumi, A. Ohya, Y. Aoki, and F. Matsuno (2007). Search for survivors buried in rubble by rescue radar with array antennas - Extraction of respiratory fluctuation. IEEE International Workshop on Safety, Security and Rescue Robotics, SSRR 2007, 1-6. DOI:10.1109/SSRR.2007.4381292.

[13] Loschonsky, M., C. Feige, O. Rogall, S. Fisun, and L. M. Reindl (2009). Detection technology for trapped and buried people. IEEE MTT-S International Microwave Workshop Wireless Sensing, Local Positioning, and RFID, 2009, IMWS 2009, 1-6. doi:10.1109/IMWS2.2009.5307879.

[14] Baboli, M., A. Sharafi, and E. Fear (2009). A framework for simulation of UWB system for heart rate detection. IEEE Trans. Biomed. Eng., 56 (9), 1200-1209.

[15] Dehmollaian, M. and K. Sarabandi (2008). Refocusing through building walls using synthetic aperture radar. IEEE Trans. Geosci. Remote Sensing, 46 (6), 1589-1599.

[16] Ajay V. K, Raghavendra Desai, Mahantesh Gawannavar and R K Nadesh. (2016). HGD: A rescue system for an alive human gesture detection in disasters management-An Experimental Study. ARPN Journal of Engineering and Applied Sciences, 11, 6826-6831.

[17] Fahed Awad, Rufaida Shamroukh (2014). Human Detection by Robotic Urban Search and Rescue Using Image Processing and Neural Networks.International Journal of Intelligence Science, 4, 39-53.

[18] Zhao, K., Wang, X., Li, Y. and Yu, X (2006) A Life-Detection System for Special Rescuing Robots. The 9th International Conference on Control, Automation, Robotics and Vision, Singapore, 1-5.

[19] Trierscheid, M., Pellenz, J., Paulus, D. and Balthasar, D. (2008). Hyperspectral Imaging for Victim Detection with Rescue Robots. Proceedings of the 2008 IEEE International Workshop on Safety, Security and Rescue Robotics, Sendai, 7-12.

[20] Jacoff, A., Weiss, B. and Messina, E. (2003). Evolution of a Performance Metric for Urban Search and Rescue Robots. Proceedings of the 2003 Performance Metrics for Intelligent Systems, Gaithersburg, 1-11.

[21] Hardeep Pal Sharma,Guna sekar.C.H, S.Adithya Kumar. (2013). Live Human Detecting Robot for Earthquake Rescue Operation. International Journal of Business Intelligent, 02, 2278-2400.

[22] Sandeep Bhatia, Hardeep Singh Dhillon and Nitin Kumar. (2011). live Human Body Detection system using an Autonomous Mobile Rescue Robot. IEEE Transactions, 11.

[23] Dandoulaki M, Andritsos F. (2007) Autonomous sensors for just-in-time information gathering in support of search and rescue in the event of building collapse Int. J. Emergency Management 4: 704-725.

[24] Murphy RR, Burke JL. (2005). Up from the rubble: Lessons learned about HRI from search and rescue. Proceed Human Factor Ergonom Soc Annu Meeting, 49, 437-441.

[25] Nourbakhsh IR, Sycara K, Koes M, Yong M, Lewis M, et al.(2005). Human-robot teaming for search and rescue. Pervasive Computing. IEEE, 4, 72-79.

[26] Huo R, Agapiou A, Bocos-Bintintan V, Brown LJ, Burns C, et al. (2011). The trapped human experiment. J Breath Res, 5, 1-12.

[27] Vijaya Krishna V (2011) Detection of Human Activity after a Natural Disaster. J Geogr Nat Disast, 1, 101. doi:10.4172/2167-0587.1000e101.

[28] R. Fuksis, M. Greitans, E. Hermanis. (2008). Motion Analysis and Remote Control System using Pyroelectric Infrared Sensors. IEEE, 6(86), 69-72.

[29] Jean Schultz, Jill L. Drury, Holly A. Yanco. (2004). Evaluation of Human-Robot Interaction Awareness in Search and Rescue. IEEE, 2327-2332.

[30]   Kun-Mu Chen, Yong Huang, Jianping Zhang and Adam Norman. (2000). Microwave Life-Detection Systems for Searching Human Subjects Under Earthquake Rubble or Behind Barrier. IEEE Transactions, Biomedical Engineering, 27, 105-114.

[31]   G.Prabhakar Reddy, M.Vijayalakshmi. (2015). IoT in mines for safety and Efficient monitoring. IJARCET, Vol 4. Issue 11.

*****

www.ingramcontent.com/pod-product-compliance
Lightning Source LLC
Chambersburg PA
CBHW071307050326
40690CB00011B/2555